$\mathcal{A}$

VOLUNTEER
YOUTH WORKER'S
GUIDE TO LEADING
A SMALL GROUP

A VOLUNTEER YOUTH WORKER'S

GUIDE TO LEADING
A SMALL GROUP

MARK OESTREICHER

bare
foot
MINISTRIES®

ISBN 978-0-8341-5130-7

Printed in the United States of America

Editor: Audra C. Marvin
Cover Design: Nathan Johnson
Interior Design: Sharon Page

Library of Congress Cataloging-in-Publication Data: 2013908402

10 9 8 7 6 5 4 3 2 1

CONTENTS

INTRODUCTION

———

Either I'm a sucker for punishment, or slightly twisted or a little bit off, or just stupid enough not to know when to quit—because I've been leading a youth ministry small group for thirty years.

Or maybe I just can't shake this calling (I've tried).

Maybe I find spending time with teenagers to be one of the most life-giving, faith-building, complacency-smashing pursuits on the face of the earth. Maybe I can't imagine not being involved with teenagers, helping them pursue Jesus, or allowing them to let Jesus pursue them.

You might not have thirty years of experience at this stuff. But if you're reading this little book, you have probably already experienced those last few reasons. Or, maybe you're new to leading a youth ministry small group. If that's the case, hold on. You could soon be in on an extraordinary secret: Youth ministry (and, specifically, leading a small group of teenagers) is maddening and glorious, unexplainable and pure, emotionally exhausting and exhilarating. Welcome to the tribe.

Either way—newbie or vet—I hope this little book will, above all else, encourage you. Yup, I hope it stirs your thinking and gives you ideas also; I hope it deepens your understanding and equips you for your next small group meeting. But mostly, I hope you hear the still, small voice of God whispering to you as you read, saying:

I love you, and I love teenagers. Thank you for caring for these precious children of mine.

WHY SMALL GROUPS?

It's easy to have youth ministry small groups be just another program alongside service projects and band practice, summer camp and Sunday school. Small groups have been the buzz-worthy programming element in youth ministry circles for the last decade or more.

That's never a good reason to launch or lead small groups.

But there are dozens, maybe even hundreds, of great reasons for putting small groups at the center of your ministry to teenagers. And if you're a small group leader, bless you because you are doing the best stuff of youth ministry. You are more a youth pastor than the highest-paid, most awesomely skilled youth pastor out there.

Maybe there are days when you feel like your investment in leading a small group is like herding cats or driving on ice or spinning your tires or yelling in space (or any other this is not effective metaphorical language you might provide). But if you don't grab hold of anything else in this short book, please ingest this: *You are making a difference. Even if there's no indication, and not one teenager ever acknowledges your efforts, God is using you—possibly in ways you will never know—in the lives of teenagers. So thank you for taking on the role of small group leader.*

Let's unpack a handful of reasons this ministry is so valuable.

The Value of Small

Americans love all things big (and if you're a Canadian, you are welcome to snidely agree; but, while you might not share the same passion for big, I've still seen how Canadians assume that big ministries are better). And we have developed a strange measuring stick for success over the last couple hundred years or so. We inherently believe that big means success. Even if you hold a healthy skepticism about this measuring stick, it's a value that permeates the church world.

But let's undermine this for a bit. I'm going to create a comparison chart, and I'll be the first to admit that there's some overstatement and generalization on this thing. Bear with me, and look for at least some truth here:

Big values compliance.	Small values uniqueness.
Big requires sameness.	Small has space for differentiation.
Big is ideally suited for broadcasting a message or rallying the troops.	Small is ideally suited for collaboration or discovery.
Big treats participants as consumers.	Small treat participants as participants.
Big is great for hype.	Small is great for owner-ship.
Big shapes a movement.	Small shapes individuals and community.
Big is stage-centric.	Small is people-centric.
Big is personality driven or program driven.	Small is relationship driven or, better yet, present.

Big, when it comes to youth ministry, has its place. I haven't given up on large-group teaching times or worship or moving a larger group toward a common goal.

But if we really want to see ownership of adolescent faith, and if we want to see faith lived out in the daily lives of teenagers, we have to get them talking and sharing honestly. That rarely happens in a larger group. In a smaller context, everyone can be known, and an environment of emotional and relational safety can be fostered.

While there are myriad ways to live into the value of small, it has to be part of the core DNA of an effective youth ministry these days. This is particularly true since today's teenagers have such a heightened need for belonging.

The Value of Consistency

A KEY VALUE FOR GREAT SMALL GROUPS IS REGULARITY.

When I write about the value of small groups, I need to clarify something: I'm not talking about spontaneously breaking up into groups that are different each time they meet. That's not necessarily a bad thing; but it lacks the consistency needed for emotional and relational safety. Instead, a key value for great small groups is regularity.

I'm a youth ministry volunteer these days (and have been for twelve years, after a couple decades as a paid youth worker). I co-lead a small group of middle school guys in my home every Wednesday night. With each group, we start with them as sixth graders and am their leader for three years (until they move into high school).

Here's what I know at the beginning of each new group of sixth graders: The entire school year will primarily be about laying the groundwork for what will happen the following two years. Not that good stuff won't happen during the year because I'm sure it will, occasionally. And, really, even laying the groundwork is good stuff. But I don't have any lofty expectations of deep spiritual conversations or amazing moments of prayer or vulnerable sharing during that first year. Maybe that will happen; but it's much more likely to occur after a good, long investment of time.

If you're working with high school students, you might arrive at that deep and honest and safe place more quickly than I can with sixth graders. But safety and belonging and being known take time.

That's why I'm committed to being there on as many Wednesday nights as possible. (The reality that I have to miss some weeks because of my work is a big reason I have a co-leader, so the group can continue to meet even when I'm out of town).

When one of the guys misses a couple weeks in a row (or when I do the same), we all suffer. There's something beautiful and powerful about a commitment to consistency, and it teaches as much or more than the curriculum and discussions you'll have with your group.

The Value of Quantity over Quality

Years ago, I worked for a highly regimented and disciplined senior pastor who had two teenage sons. Both of his sons were good kids (in fact, as adults, both of these guys are now pastors themselves). This pastor was one of those people who was always looking for a new system to save him time, improve his golf swing, leverage his skills, or increase his efficiency. To that end, he instituted a new system for spending time with his two sons: the weekly appointment.

QUANTITY TIME IS THE ONLY PATH TO QUALITY TIME.

Now, as a parent, I think there's great value in a weekly appointment with my kids (though I don't think I'd use that term). But this dad was an all-in kind of guy, and when the hour or ninety minutes he had blocked out for one of his sons came around, he expected to dive deep into a conversation about what was really going on in their lives and minds and hearts.

After a couple weeks of this new system, his high school son complained: *Dad, I'm not one of your projects! You can't just schedule good conversations with me. Good conversations will happen when they happen. I'm happy to spend time with you, but don't always expect that what I need at that moment is a deep conversation. Sometimes I just want to hang out with you.*

To his credit, this senior pastor/dad had *an aha* moment, which he shared with me: *My sons need quantity time, not just quality time.*

Yes! There's a great truth in this. And it's counterintuitive to most of us because, in our busyness, we've all heard lots of messages about maximizing the moment and how quality is so much more important than quantity.

But teenagers don't work that way. They're not things or projects. They're real people, and sometimes they just want to hang out.

With that in mind, embrace the value that quantity time is the only path to quality time. In other words, if you're not willing to invest time and presence regularly, consistently, over time (years!), you'll rarely get to those amazing moments of deep transforming dialogue, life application, and honesty.

The Value of the Long View

Akin to the last value, it's critical that good youth workers have a long view. Life change rarely happens quickly. Sure, there are condensed, intense times—like mission trips or camps or when a significant pain or tragedy is experienced—that provide a context for significant growth and decisions. But more commonly, transformation takes time.

This is really one of the most challenging aspects of any ministry that involves humans (as opposed to, like, helping in the parking lot ministry). People are messy and complex, and change takes time. Because teenagers are in such a massive period of change anyhow, we often don't see the results of our investment in real time. For this reason, if you're going to look for results, you should look at your students ten years from now.

And, even if you don't have the ability or patience to wait around ten years for results, great small group leaders still hold onto that perspective. We understand that the students we're working with won't stay the way they are (thank God!). We understand that they're on a journey and that who they're becoming is just as important (if not more important) than who they are today.

Veteran youth worker Jim Hancock wrote a book for parents several years ago with a title that really captured my imagination. It was called Raising Adults. It was a book about parenting teenagers, but even the title cast a vision for the value of the long haul.

You will be sorely misinformed and misled if the only indicators of how you're doing as a small group leader are things like:

- Whether this or that youth group kid shows up
- If anyone says something about what a great leader you are or thanks you in any way
- Whether each and every meeting of your small group includes a deep and honest time of sharing
- If the students in your group remember what you talked about last week

SPEAKING OF VALUES . . .

All the methodology in the world, all the brilliance in forming questions, all the listening skills, all the knowledge and understanding of teenagers, all the theological training you could possibly want . . .

. . . won't do you much good if the small group values are misguided or mushy.

Let me give you an actual story of a small group leader. This is real, and it's preposterously extreme, but it proves this point.

John was a high school junior, and his small group leader was in his mid-twenties. His small group was made up of juniors and seniors in high school, all guys. John loved hanging out with this group and felt really close to his small group leader. They all *did life* together, at the church and on their own turf. Sounds like what we're hoping for, right?

Wrong.

When each of the guys in the group turned eighteen (and yes, this was a church small group), their small group leader took them to a strip club, bought them alcohol, and got drunk with them.

GOALS ARE FINE, BUT WITHOUT VALUES TO GUIDE US, WE DON'T HAVE A WAY OF KNOWING IF OUR GOALS ARE ANY GOOD.

Uh . . . yeah. So, clearly, that small group leader had a different set of values than you and I might have for our groups (I hope so!).

We talk a lot about goals in youth ministry and the church (and business, for that matter). And goals are fine, but without values to guide us, we don't have a way of knowing if our goals are any good.

I can't tell you exactly what values you should have for your small group because they should reflect your church, local context, and youth ministry at large, in addition to the uniquenesses that you bring to small group leadership. But you might think about values like:

- *We believe that wrestling with questions can be just as important as reaching answers.*

- *We are committed to a small group where every student is known, called by name, and welcomed.*

- *We think that meeting regularly and consistently is critical to the relational context we're trying to foster.*

- *We are confident that Jesus is the Savior, and I (the small group leader) am not. I am incapable of changing lives.*

In fact, how about I give you the values of the small groups from the church where I volunteer (not because you should adopt all of them as your own but merely as an example). These values are stated as a covenant that each participant signs at the start of each school year (leaders and students both).

- **Consistent Participation**

  Proverbs 20:6, 18:24

  I will regularly attend my small group and participate in the discussion. In the event that I must miss a meeting, I will communicate that info to my group leader(s).

- **Accepting**

  Proverbs 14:21

  I know that being part of this small group will require time, patience, love, and forgiveness. I am committed to not being judgmental but instead to help affirm and cheerlead my peers as we aim to be more and more like Jesus.

- **Teachable**

  Proverbs 12:15, 27:17

  I want to grow in my spiritual maturity and in the image of God. As a result, I am committed to being teachable, realizing I have some growing to do. That's why I joined this group anyway. I am willing to walk with people in their brokenness and need others to do this with me.

- **Authentic**

  Proverbs 12:17

  I will be honest and open with my life, being truthful at all times. I realize accountability is pointless if I lie.

- **Confidential**

  Proverbs 20:19

I will honor the words and lives of my small group by not communicating what we discuss here with others outside this group. I expect my small group to do the same for me. I also understand that my small group leader may break this confidentiality to seek advice or help from others outside our group if they need some counsel to help me or feel that my health or safety are in danger.

With those five values stated (and discussed and agreed to), not only do I as a leader have both a direction in which to head and a sense of the culture we're trying to create, but so, likewise, do all the students.

WHAT'S THE POINT?

Years ago, I was hosting a youth ministry conversation at an event in England, with a panel of the leading voices in British youth ministry. I described a handful of different approaches to youth ministry and asked the panel to respond. I remember very clearly that Pete Ward, a godfather of youth ministry in the UK, sighed and said, "There are really only two kinds of youth ministry: inside-out youth ministries and outside-in youth ministries." He meant simply that there were those more interested in discipleship and those more passionate about evangelism.

While I remember thinking—and still think—that there's more complexity and nuance to the differences in youth ministries, Pete's words have stuck with me over the years because they do seem to sum up the vast majority of youth groups.

Characterizing the passion and focus of your small group can be really helpful. It's important to know why you exist, why you bother meeting together. You might come up with your own description or some combination of descriptions; but here are four approaches to small groups I've seen most often. Which one resonates most with you? Which one is most reflective of the approach you're currently using?

Education

Traditionally, youth ministry sprang up out of the Sunday school movement, which often became the Christian education department of a church. That name summarizes the approach well: Small groups with this focus are primarily concerned with educating teenagers in the Christian faith.

If you're not sure whether this is your approach, consider the content and form. In other words, if the content (at least what you hope the content would be!) is focused on transferring truth to students, helping them to increase in knowledge, then this is probably your approach. And if your small group times are primarily teacher-centric or focused on the information being given by the small group leader, it's a strong indicator that your group has an education focus.

That's not a bad thing. It can, however, end up feeling a lot like school to teenagers and be a turn off. The dark side of this approach is that it can tend to focus only on the minds of students and the information they can grasp. But living as a follower of Jesus is a whole-person activity—mind, heart, emotion, and behavior.

Bible Study

Closely related to the previous focus, a Bible study focus is mostly educational. But, instead of relying primarily on instruction about beliefs, this purpose is more interested in helping teenagers discover and understand biblical truth by (ready for it?) actually digging into the Bible.

THE BIBLE IS GOD'S PRIMARY MEANS OF REVELATION TO US.

Here's what's great about this approach: The Bible is God's primary means of revelation to us, and most Christian teenagers today are fairly clueless about the Bible, the truths of Scripture, and even the stories that speak to us. Bible reading among Christians has declined significantly in the past few decades. In fact, a recent Gallup poll showed that 20 percent (1 in 5) Bible readers have stopped reading the Bible over the span of a generation. And the Reveal study conducted by Willowcreek found that only 1 in 5 churchgoers say they're getting the help they need understanding the Bible.

Biblica (formerly International Bible Society) suggests, from their study of this problem, that there are three reasons for this decline:

- We read the Bible in fragments. We read a verse here, most of a chapter there, but never the whole story.
- We read the Bible without context. We know it's an ancient collection of books from a culture different

from our own, but we don't do the work to bridge the gap between the world of the Bible and our world today. As a result, much of it doesn't make sense and leaves readers frustrated.

• We read the Bible in isolation. We've turned Bible reading into a solo activity, which was never the practice for the original audience.

A Bible study–focused small group has the opportunity to reverse these three damaging trends by offering the opposite of each. This focus can be amazing, particularly when it helps teenagers engage Scripture. But what I've seen is that most small groups that say they are Bible study-focused are really an educational model with a teacher dispensing information and very little actual interaction with Scripture for the students.

Community/Therapeutic

This is probably the most common approach or focus for youth ministry small groups. The hope is to create an authentic community, a place where students can be honest about the real stuff of their lives, including the integration of their faith into daily life.

I added the word *therapeutic* to this description not as a negative but as an indication that these kinds of groups often provide a kind of semi-therapy for the trauma teenagers experience.

An example: Recently in my sixth-grade boys small group, during our first regular meeting together, we were getting to know each other. I had each of the guys share a bit about their homes (parents, siblings, pets). One of the guys shared that he has an older brother whom he hasn't seen in a few months because his brother is addicted to crystal meth. He even shared that his brother first started using crystal meth on his (the sixth-grade boy's) birthday. While he knew these weren't connected, it was clearly a serious point of pain for him. The group stopped their fidgeting and noisemaking and focused on the boy who was sharing. They asked him sensitive questions and showed genuine care. Then the whole group prayed for him, including a couple of the other boys. This experience would have had therapeutic value for that guy (as well as drawn him a bit more into the potential community of our little group).

There's great value in this approach to small groups. In fact, it's probably the purpose that I most closely align with in my own small group leadership style. At the beginning of a new year, I send an email to the parents of my new sixth-grade guys, going over some administrative details. The email I sent this year included these words:

What we're trying to accomplish

Our grow group isn't a Bible study, per se, though we will look at the Bible. With young teens who are moving into a developmental stage with more change than any other time of their lives, except the first two years of life, our group is more about creating a safe place to be known, to share honestly about questions and doubts, hopes and fears, all under the banner of learning what it means to live as young men following Jesus. One of the reasons I love working with this age is that they really will go from being boys to young men over the span of the three years.

To that end, we'll usually have a curriculum of some sort that we're using, something to provide a context for spiritual discussions. But the emphasis will rarely be on information or knowledge and will be more focused on application and faith ownership.

We'll break our time roughly into three segments each week: about thirty minutes of catching up with each other, thirty to forty minutes of a lesson (a guided discussion, really), and twenty to thirty minutes of snacking and goofing around. The relational element of our time isn't just silliness for its own sake. We need to build relational strength in order to accomplish what we're hoping for. In fact, I often think of this first year as laying the relational groundwork for the amazing discussions that will take place in the seventh and eighth grades.

The caution on this approach is that it's easy to get lazy and have the group time amount to nothing more than shooting the breeze. Without some focused intentionality, particularly in bringing up spiritual subjects, the group could end up enjoying each other but not accomplishing more than a fun night of hanging out each week.

Mini Youth Group

Most youth ministry small groups focus in on one purpose (like those listed above). But the mini youth group approach throws the net wider. This approach views the small group as a youth ministry of its own, with the small group leader acting as a youth pastor, of sorts.

Think of all the functions and purposes of a youth group. You might create a list that includes worship, teaching, evangelism, discipleship, fellowship, serving, and more. Well, the mini youth group approach to small groups embraces all of those.

This is probably the most rare, but it's worth considering. Think of the impact on your group of going on a mission trip as a group. Or what if worship (not just singing, by the way) became a regular part of your small group? In a sense, this kind of small group attempts to live out what it means to be the church in the context of their small group. And that can be very powerful.

WHAT DOES CHANGE LOOK LIKE?

———

Before we move into some structural stuff and a bunch
of other tangible ideas, let's take a minute to talk about
spiritual transformation. That's why we have small groups,
right? Whatever our approach, we hope to see change take
place in the lives of teenagers. We hope to host the work of
the Holy Spirit bringing transformation to their very beings.

So what's that look like?

A number of years ago, I was with a group of seasoned
youth workers, putting together the content for a day of
training for volunteer youth workers. Part of our training
day was focused on this question of spiritual transformation. At some point in our conversation, someone asked
each of us to take a few minutes to make some notes about
the most significant times of spiritual transformation in
our own stories. Then each of us took a few minutes to
tell these stories. Someone stood at a wall with a bunch of
sticky notes and jotted down themes.

When we had a wall full of sticky notes, we spent some time looking them over, searching for themes. And an interesting pattern emerged. We discovered that significant spiritual transformation seemed to occur most often in four contexts:

Victory and Success

When a teenager experiences any success in life, it's cause for celebration. Sure, this can include public successes, like scoring a goal in a soccer game or some sort of academic achievement. But success or victory in any area of life—particularly if it includes a sense of overcoming obstacles—can provide a context for change.

> **GREAT SMALL GROUP LEADERS ARE ALWAYS WATCHING FOR WINS, ALWAYS LISTENING FOR VICTORY.**

For some teenagers, just showing up at your small group is a victory. For that one girl, resisting the urge to gossip is a huge success. For that one guy, speaking a word of encouragement to someone is a big win.

Great small group leaders are always watching for wins, always listening for victory. And great small group leaders are intentional about stopping to celebrate (even if that means a quiet comment on the side or a text message later that evening).

There's a memorable line from the 1981 classic movie Chariots of Fire, when Christian runner Eric Liddell says,

"When I run, I feel [God's] pleasure." We need to point students to Christ when they experience victory and success. Help them feel God's pleasure. Point out how this success reveals something about who God made them to be. That kind of understanding can be extremely life shaping.

Perspective-Altering Experiences

We've all had those moments when the scales fall from our eyes and we see things in a new light. At least in that moment, you fully believe that you could never go back to seeing things the old way.

When the old woman in the village you're working in on a mission trip says that she thinks you might be angels sent from heaven. When you experience a deep sense of belonging and acceptance with a few friends who've just forgiven you for a deep hurt you caused. When you feel a tangible sense of God's presence during a time of worship or sense God speaking to you more clearly than you've ever experienced before. When you see, for the first time, the impact of your sin on the life of another. When you first heard someone other than a relative say the words, "I love you" in a way that took your breath away.

These kind of perspective-altering experiences bump into the trajectory of our stories and alter the course. Even if the recalibration is a small degree, it can greatly impact the long-term direction of our lives.

Psychologists call this *disequilibration*. That's the ten-dollar word for being off balance. That sense of being off balance doesn't have to be literal, of course. It can merely mean that our normal understanding of "the way things are" no longer makes sense. Our current world-view is no longer sufficient. Our understanding of God is revealed as inadequate.

This is the great stuff of youth ministry. And anyone who's been around youth ministry for a while has seen this many, many times. It often happens on camps and retreats. It almost always occurs on mission trips. Most of our ministries are at least subconsciously aware of this reality and don't miss the opportunity to provide or capitalize on these moments of new perspective.

But what would it look like to see perspective-altering experiences as a part of your small group? Even if the experiences themselves don't take place in the confines of the group, we have the opportunity to dive deep into the wonderful space of disequilibration and participate in the reorientation that can flow forward.

Community

We all have, deeply embedded in our design, desires to be known and to belong. In real community, we experience a satisfaction of those desires. This isn't about being needy. Instead, these desires are a reflection of our being made in the image of God. And deep spiritual transformation often occurs in the context of community. It's the safety of being known and unconditionally loved and accepted that provides the rich soil for internal change.

Of course, it's not the community itself that produces the spiritual change (any more than successes and per-spective-altering experiences can make change happen). Change is God's work, through the Holy Spirit. But community (and the other contexts listed here) provides a softening of the heart and openness of the mind and a willing-ness of the spirit that invites God's transforming work.

Since we were made for com-munity, it only makes sense that most of us experience real, long-term, life-altering change when in community. And to that end, we don't just gather in our small groups to pursue an educational information dump. Students aren't ATMs where we can make deposits of pithy spiritual truths, hoping to withdraw them later. Instead, like all the Jesus followers who came before us, we work out what it means to live as a Christian in community.

STUDENTS AREN'T ATMS WHERE WE CAN MAKE DEPOSITS OF PITHY SPIRITUAL TRUTHS, HOPING TO WITHDRAW THEM LATER.

Pain and Failure

Remember how I discovered these four contexts in the working group of youth workers, sharing our own stories of significant spiritual transformation? There was some ranking to these things. Victory and

Success was a minor player, actually. Community was often alongside whatever else provided the window of opportunity. Perspective-Altering Experiences was a biggie; we each had stories that fit this.

But the most significant context for change is often (and was for that group) the learning that can come from pain and failure.

WE DON'T OR CAN'T OR AT LEAST SHOULDN'T PROGRAM FOR [PAIN AND FAILURE].

When I look back over my own life and spiritual growth, I can unequivocally confirm that pain caused by wrong done to me and pain caused by my own stupid choices have consistently brought about more deep change than all the other contexts combined.

Of course, pain and failure can bring on plenty of non-growth results also. That's why we have to walk alongside teenagers in their pain and failure, providing a grace-filled, loving, safe place to process that stuff and point in a new direction (while always pointing to Jesus).

This context is unique from the others in one particular way: We don't or can't or at least shouldn't program for it. You can provide opportunities for success, program perspective-altering experiences, and work intentionally toward community. But you'd be a very, very bad youth worker if you actually built in pain and failure, right?

Instead, our role is to be hyper-alert and responsive. Our role is to ask questions and be relationally present to teenagers so we'll be aware of the times of pain and failure that absolutely will, without doubt, show up.

THINKING STRUCTURE

Time to get to some practical stuff. When I talk with youth workers about small groups, there are a handful of questions that commonly come up. Let's dive into them but with the perspective that there isn't one right answer. The best approach to small groups is the one you and a group of spiritually minded people have prayerfully discerned to be contextually appropriate for who you and your group are, where you're located, what makes the most sense given logistical details, and how the Holy Spirit leads you.

Single Gender vs. Mixed

I'm a fan of separating genders, guys and girls. Not all the time, mind you. Developmentally, it's critical that we create good and safe places for teenagers to try on relational connections across gender lines without all the cultural pressure (common at school and the mall) of hooking up.

But the best stuff of youth ministry, when it comes down to it, happens when teenagers are able to be the most honest and present in every way. And, adding the other gender into the mix colors everything. So I like to separate genders at crucial times.

Particularly, I think it's wise to have single-gender small groups. The whole point of small groups, after all, is to create a safe place where students are known. In the context of being known, we hope they will honestly and wholly enter into dialogue and collaborative discernment and verbal wrestling with truth, all of which requires a level of vulnerability. Single-gender groups just grease the rails.

Splitting Middle School and High School

Let's face it: A seventh grader and an eleventh grader are *not* in the same developmental space. And their experiences of life aren't just apples and oranges; it's more like apples and orangutans.

Let's say you're having an honest conversation with a group of middle school and high school guys about dating and sexuality. You're talking about the temptation to fool around physically. On one end of the spectrum, you've got guys with guilt and experience and real-world stories of times they've struggled, times they've failed, and times they've resisted. Of course, not all older teens are experienced in this area, but they all certainly understand it at a deeply personal level.

Then you've got a sixth grader in the group. And he's thinking, *What? Are you talking about kissing? You guys have actually kissed a girl!?!* Apples and orangutans.

Of course, there's some great stuff that can come out of a small group that has both young teens and older teens. The young teens have an opportunity to learn from the older guys, and the older guys have an opportunity to mentor the younger guys, thinking about how their lives are having an impact by the way they live and what they say.

As a rule, I'm a fan of separating middle schoolers and high schoolers in small groups, if you can. But this question (or the answer to it) often boils down to an issue of practicality. If you only have four guys in your whole youth group (middle school and high school combined), then it's a bit tough to have two separate groups. So capitalize on the potential strengths of a combined group and make the best of it. Make sure you're intentional about having conversations with the older guys apart from the younger ones at times. (I'm just using guys as an example here, since, well, I'm a guy, but the same goes for girls.)

Single Grade vs. Mixed Grades

So, then, what if your youth ministry is large enough to have separate middle school and high school small groups and large enough to have multiple groups of each? Should you continue to keep them as homogeneous as possible, narrowing each group to one grade, or mix it up a bit?

There are advantages to both approaches. The biggest reason I like separating grades when you can, into grade-specific small groups, is that it allows for a small group leader and a particular small group of students to journey together over multiple years, which enormously increases all the good things about a small group: community, safety, belonging, being known.

For example, I'm on my seventh year as a small group leader. When I take on a new group of sixth-grade boys, I'm making a three-year commitment. I've taken two groups of guys through a three-year cycle now and have just started with a third group of sixth-grade boys.

But our high school ministry has traditionally used mixed-grade groups. They find it's helpful to all the students in the group to have a little variety of ages.

Homogeneous vs. Affinity vs. Other

What if grades and genders aren't the best means of dividing up into small groups? In this current world of splintered youth culture, could we make a case for forming groups in a different way?

I was talking with a youth pastor friend who was in the midst of rethinking the structure of his small groups. He found that he had a majority of students whose maturity and interests were ideally suited for a small group using the community approach I described before. But he had a smaller percentage who really longed for an actual Bible study as the core of their small group experience. As a result, he was thinking of offering two different kinds of small groups and was just wrestling with how to communicate this without making it sound like the Bible study groups were somehow better or what one would choose if one wanted to be a "good kid."

In the midst of this conversation, he mentioned a third group of students. Living in southern California, he had a group of students—mostly boys—who were avid surfers. And there was one adult leader, also a surfer, who unofficially rallied those guys to surf together. They often hung out on the beach afterward or went to get breakfast burritos. My friend was struggling with the fact that the guys in this crowd resisted coming to the midweek small groups. So we started talking about making the surfing group a small group of its own.

In this sense, the small groups would be formed more around affinities than markers of age or grade.

Another example: Another youth pastor friend worked in a church with massive racial diversity (a great thing!). As the ministry grew in its impact with African American and Latino students, they realized that their ministry approach to small groups—which had always been single grade and gender—didn't translate well to the relational structures of those communities. Where his white and Asian students tended to have friends in the same grade as themselves, the African American and Latino students were just as likely to have signifi-

BE INTENTIONAL ABOUT WHATEVER YOU DO.

cant friendships two or three years younger or older than themselves. When he realized he was forcing these kids into a structure that didn't mirror the natural relational web of the students who were coming, he made a significant change in order to reflect the values of the community.

As you can see from these examples, and as I wrote earlier, this comes down to discernment. What's best for your community? What's the Holy Spirit calling you to do? Be intentional about whatever you do.

UNDERSTANDING GENDER DIFFERENCES

Teenage girls form relational bonds around verbalization. Another way to say that: Girls like to talk. And that process of talking is often the glue that cements relationships.

If you're leading a girls' small group, it's unlikely you'll struggle to get them to talk. In fact, the average teenage girl uses twenty thousand words a day. That's a lot of talking!

Teenage guys, on average, use about five thousand words a day. And I'm pretty sure that at least half of those are actually grunts and other sounds that barely qualify as words. Sure, there are plenty of verbal guys. But the guy code teaches them a few cultural norms they're supposed to embody:

1. Even if I'm struggling with something, I'm supposed to present an *I'm fine* front.
2. Even if what I'm trying to accomplish could never be done on my own, I'm supposed to present an *I don't need any help* front.
3. It is not acceptable (and will hurt my social standing) to exhibit any emotion other than anger.
4. And, maybe more than anything else, I will not talk too much, if at all.

Teenage guys form relational bonds around doing things together. This creates an interesting challenge for guys' small group leaders, who often approach (or are expected to approach) small groups with an emphasis on verbalization. Once a group becomes safe for guys and a norm of talking honestly gets established, you'll find that guys can totally dive into a small group based on sharing things through talking. But at first it can be a bit more challenging.

So, do something together. Duh.

LEADING GREAT DISCUSSIONS

Let's dive into leading discussions; because, when it comes down to it, that's how great small groups function. And the role of a great leader isn't first and foremost in the dispensing of wisdom or in the artful arrangement of the room but in the ability to guide and focus a conversation.

Plan

Great conversations in the context of a group are often spontaneous. You don't have to be a small group leader for long before you discover this. But that shouldn't be an excuse for a lack of planning.

Here's what I've found: When I have a newer small group, where the members don't know each other very well yet and don't feel totally safe with each other, I need more planning and preparation. The safer the group gets and the more the teenagers in the group know each other (and feel known), the less preparation I need. In fact, being overly dependent on a particular curriculum plan can actually reduce the potential good stuff that naturally springs forth from a safe group in which everyone is known and valued.

But we need some rails to run on, or the group can easily spin off into idle chatter that doesn't dig into the real stuff of life and truth. My middle school guys' small group could easily fill our times with talk of video games and girls and school and sports. These subjects all offer great opportunity to have deeper conversations, by the way. But without some guidance and shaping, the conversation will rarely dip below the surface.

ALL THE PLANNING IN THE WORLD WON'T MAKE YOU A GREAT YOUTH MINISTRY SMALL GROUP LEADER IF YOU'RE NOT FLEXIBLE.

Winging it is a classic youth ministry skill, but it's rarely the best route to depth. So have a plan, and put some thought and study into preparing that plan ahead of time. Think through your theme, Scripture passages you'd like to look at, a story of your own, and—maybe most importantly—those first few questions to get a conversation up and running.

Flexibility

All the planning in the world won't make you a great youth ministry small group leader if you're not flexible.

A horribly obvious case study: Years ago I was a youth pastor in Pasadena, California, the year we had deadly fires sweep through the mountains just above us. The fires dipped down in the neighborhoods near the mountains, devastating homes and lives. On the worst day of the fires, our group met. Our normal meeting space wasn't available that evening for some reason, and we met in an upstairs room that had floor-to-ceiling windows facing in the direction of the fires. We could watch as homes burst into flames, as fire trucks raced about, and as an apocalyptic vision literally played out in front of our eyes. I even had a student show up that evening whose family had lost their home that day. Her parents were scrambling to figure out where they were going to sleep that night and had dropped their daughter off at youth group to give her a little break from madness. We had few students show up, and it was basically a small group—about eight or ten teenagers.

Ready to be horrified by my over-the-top obvious stupidity? I stuck to my lesson plan. I was wonderfully prepared with a great lesson and conversation on some particular subject or scripture. And I didn't flex. I didn't address the obvious. I didn't create space for conversation about the pain and questions on every single student's mind. What a dork.

I'm sure you're not as lame as that. But when we're effectively prepared and have in our heads a particular vision of how the small group time will play out, all of us are capable of a rigidity that robs everyone of the stuff we most hope for. Really, when we aren't flexible, we can miss the movement of the Holy Spirit.

Understand Learning

Don't think of learning as the acquisition of head knowledge. Real learning gets embodied and shows up as a new understanding or perspective that shapes how we live and the choices we make.

But here's where we often make a fatal mistake: We assume learners (in this case, teenagers in our small group) can go from information to lived-out truth. But there are a few more critical steps in the process. And without some intentionality, we can easily miss these steps, decreasing the potential impact of our small group.

UNLESS THE LEARNER PLACES VALUE ON EITHER THE SUBJECT OR THE PROCESS, THERE'S NO CHANCE SHE'S APPLYING IT TO HER LIFE.

Learning does start with data and recall. That can be a Bible verse or a truth or a question or an experience. But that's only a starting point. The second step in the learning process is valuing. Unless the learner places value on either the subject or the process, there's no chance she's applying it to her life.

We'd love to think that all teenagers would naturally attach value to our brilliant small group discussions of the book of Numbers. But even the most titillating of subjects (some have sarcastically suggested that the top three for teenagers are sex, the end times, and sex in the end times) will only provide enough interest for a majority of your group to attach value.

But here's the good news: Teenagers can attach value to the conversation because they care about the relationship. In other words, if they feel known and accepted, if they belong and care about that, they will attach value to the learning process even if they're not particularly ecstatic about the actual subject.

The third step in the learning process is speculation. This is the act of asking *What if?* As an adult, you do this naturally once you've attached value. You're doing it right now (hopefully) as you're reading this book. But here's the rub: Teenagers are notoriously bad at speculation, particularly if they're young or middle teens. Speculation requires abstract thinking. And, while teenagers have the capacity for abstract thought, they haven't exercised it enough to be fluent. As a result, one of our primary strategies for effective small group leadership with teenagers is to ask speculation questions.

The fourth step in the learning process is trying. This is the act of trying on new behaviors. Sometimes we can enter into this step during a small group, but more commonly, the trying step becomes another act of speculation, tied with a decision to experiment with a new behavior or belief.

Finally, after trying on a new behavior or idea or belief, and finding it to be worthy, the learner moves to doing, the final step. Now the idea or experience from the starting point is a part of the learner and factors into future learning.

One more thing to point out here: There's a gap in the process between speculation and trying. I call it the knowing/doing gap because everything prior to the gap is cognitive. Action comes after the gap. Our goal is to help students cross that gap.

The Hidden Curriculum and the Null Curriculum

The phrases in this subhead are, admittedly, fancy educational terms. But they're worth you being aware of them because they teach just as much as the stuff you intend to teach (what we might call the explicit curriculum).

The *hidden curriculum* embodies all the variables and values of your small group time that aren't directly tied to your explicit curriculum.

- Who gets to talk when.
- What distractions you'll allow and what distractions you won't allow.
- Your facial expressions and body language when group members are speaking (particularly when they're saying things that push your buttons).
- How the room and seating are arranged.
- What you say and do before and after you dive into the explicit curriculum.

Here's an example: If you regularly allow for one particular teenager to interrupt but regularly shut down another, you are teaching something clearly about your preferences, which can have an enormous impact on both of those students and everyone else in the group.

The *null curriculum* is, quite simply, all the stuff you don't or won't talk about. For instance, if you never address sexuality—either because it makes you uncomfortable or because you think it's a subject better dealt with in another context—you implicitly teach your group that sexuality is a taboo subject that shouldn't be talked about anywhere. Of course, teenagers will talk about sexuality; so, in essence, you're teaching them that they should talk about it anywhere other than at church or in a Christian context. The follow-up to that understanding, then, for teenagers, would be that the Bible doesn't really have anything relevant to say about this subject that is so ready and present to their daily lives.

ASKING GREAT QUESTIONS

If you're going to lead great conversations, you need to become a student of questions. Great small group leaders understand different kinds of questions and how to intersperse them at the right times. We've all been in learning contexts where the leader has merely asked one kind of question over and over and over again. You know how brain and soul numbing that can be.

As we look at these different kinds of questions, remember this: Variety is the key. Mix it up.

Polar Questions

Polar questions, as their name implies, are really cold. I'm kidding. Actually, a polar question is the official name for a yes/no question. In a broader sense, a polar question can be any question that only has two possible answers.

Polar questions should be used sparingly in youth ministry small groups. Once in a while, polar questions can be helpful. I can think of two ways they can be helpful. First, the occasional use of a list of yes/no questions can act as an interesting introduction to a subject.

For instance, if I were going to lead a conversation about lying, I might start with a quick list of these polar questions:

- Have you ever lied about feeling sick to avoid going to school or doing a chore?
- Have you ever lied about what you brought in your lunch so your friend wouldn't try to steal it?
- Have you ever lied to a teacher about why you didn't get your homework finished?
- Have you ever lied to a friend about something you heard about him or her because you thought the truth would hurt?

The second good use of polar questions is when the response is followed immediately by, "Why?" or, "Talk about that." In either of these good uses of polar questions, the strength is in the follow-up, the conversation and thoughts behind the yes or no.

Information Questions

Information questions highlight particular aspects of what was just observed or discussed, in order to emphasize or draw out a fact. These questions can very quickly feel like a quiz or like school in general; so, like polar questions, we need to use them sparingly. But information questions are particularly helpful when digging into a Bible passage or story. Use them intentionally to focus on aspects of the passage that you want to be sure get noticed.

Let's say you're looking at the story of Shadrach, Meshach, and Abednego. It could be helpful to ask:

- What did the guys do, specifically, that got them in trouble?
- What did they say to the king when he threatened to throw them into the fiery furnace?
- What did the king notice when the guys were in the furnace?

Understanding Questions

Understanding questions can, at first, sound a lot like information questions. The difference is that understanding questions require some subjectivity, whereas information questions are purely objective.

Using the example of Shadrach, Meshach, and Abednego, some good understanding questions might be:

- What was really behind the King's willingness to build the statue?
- Why do you think the guys weren't afraid?
- Whom do you think the fourth person was walking around in the furnace?

Implication/Speculation Questions

Remember the learning process I wrote about a few pages ago? There was that step in the process called speculation. It's the learning requirement that we think about

TEENAGERS AREN'T NATURALLY GOOD AT SPECULATION.

what this information or idea or truth might mean for us. Remember, since teenagers aren't naturally good at speculation, it's imperative that we pepper our small group conversations with great speculation questions. Like understanding questions, these are subjective, not objective. But, rather than being focused on the content or passage or idea itself, these questions bring out implications for the individual teenagers in your group.

For Shad, Shach, and Benny (thanks, VeggieTales!), you might ask:

- What would you have done if you were in their shoes when the "call to worship" sounded?
- What would you have been feeling when you were brought up to the edge of the furnace?
- What are some ways that you're asked to "bow down" to idols and objects of worship that aren't God?
- How can you have the courage to take a stand like Shad, Shach, and Benny?

Application Questions

Back to that learning process again: Remember the knowing/doing gap? On one side, the learning process included recall, value, and speculation. On the other side of the gap were trying and doing. Application questions are intended to bridge that gap. We might speculate about what bridging the gap (applying this truth to my life) might look like prior to the gap; but application questions ask for specific action on the other side.

For the three who would not bow:

- What's a real situation in your life where you've been asked to go against what you believe and what God wants for you? What can you do this week to take a stand on that?
- What will you do to put yourself in a place, like Shadrach, Meshach, and Abednego, where you'll have the courage to stand for what you know is right?

THINGS THAT MIGHT HELP

Finally, here are a handful of little bonus ideas. Some of these variables might not be yours to decide (like where you meet), but most of these ideas are things you can consider injecting into your small group to add strength, community, and safety.

Place

Where you meet is very much a part of that hidden curriculum I wrote about earlier. And, if your youth ministry small group is like so many others, the place you meet might be the corner of an otherwise busy room or a hot, windowless little room that doubles as the church janitor's storage for cleaning products. Good luck with that.

If you do have any say in where your group meets, consider a couple factors. First, consistency really helps. If you can meet in the same place every week (or every time you meet), the familiarity will reduce distractions and increase safety. A familiar space feels like our place, even if you have to share it with a dozen other groups throughout the week. But I gotta tell ya, meeting in a home is so good and offers up the opportunity for intimacy that can be challenging in a cinderblock room at a church.

Also, privacy is a big deal (this is why meeting in the corner of an otherwise busy room is so *difficult!*). You want to create a space where, over time, the students in your group can be fully present and fully honest. And if they're always wondering whether someone is going to overhear them, the chances of creating that kind of safe space are minimal. I'd always choose a smelly but private janitor's closet over the corner of a room that has four other small groups meeting in it.

Multiple Leaders

I realize it's tough for most youth ministries to get enough adult volunteers to have more than one leader in each small group. But the benefits are so numerous, it's truly worth pursuing. If your youth ministry can't provide this for you, go out and recruit your own co-leader!

I have a co-leader in my small group right now. His name is Gary. We trade weeks in terms of primary preparation and leading, but both of us jump in to help the discussion. If we have a guy who needs a little side conversation (either because something deeply personal that would be inappropriate for the group comes up, or—more commonly for us—because one of the guys needs a little chat to remind him of our group covenant), one of us can continue leading the group while the other one steps outside. If one of us has to miss a week because of our day jobs or because of family needs or because of sickness, the group doesn't have to take the week off. And the reality is, Gary and I are different people, and we relate to the guys in different ways. That's a wonderful strength in our group.

I've loved working with younger co-leaders at times too, either high school students (since I lead a middle school group) or young adults. I find that the younger leader brings things I could never bring to the mix (energy, availability, cultural knowledge, a surrogate big brother or big sister relationship); and I bring things to the mix that would be more difficult for them (maturity and life experience, broader knowledge, a surrogate parent relationship).

The bottom line is, I couldn't more strongly encourage you to pursue having two leaders for your small group.

Variety and Breaks

My small group has a basic format. But I know that if we keep to that exact format every week, it will start to get stale. Adding variety keeps things fresh. A few years back, I lived in a house with a great pool and spa. So once a month, we had small group swim night. We had a different flow of time on those nights that still included a shorter time of sharing and prayer, which happened in the hot tub! I don't live in that house anymore, so I try to mix it up in other ways: taking the guys to Starbucks or an ice cream place occasionally or meeting in some other location.

And, as much as I value consistency and longevity, I know I need breaks if I'm going to stay in this for the long haul. I make no apologies about taking a week off here and there, particularly at holidays. And my groups take the entire summer off (though I stay in touch with the guys and schedule at least one get-together over the summer months).

AS MUCH AS I VALUE CONSISTENCY AND LONGEVITY, I KNOW I NEED BREAKS IF I'M GOING TO STAY IN THIS FOR THE LONG HAUL.

Snacks

Maybe you think this is juvenile. Or maybe you think having a snack is a waste of time and attention that could best be spent in other ways. All I can tell you is that gathering over a meal is a fast track to community, and having a snack is a mini version of that.

You don't have to bear it on your own, by the way I pass out a snack rotation schedule (I send it to the parents) and ask that each week a different small group participant bring a snack for the group and a decaffeinated beverage for everyone.

Gifts

A word to the women: Yeah, you probably already totally understand the power of gifts. They don't have to be expensive or even store bought. 'Nuff said.

A bunch of words to the men: You might think that giving gifts to your small group of guys is weird. You are wrong. I mean, sure, it could be weird, depending on the gift. But the once-in-a-while gift can have a huge impact on guys and tells them in no uncertain terms that you were thinking about them when you weren't with them and that you care about them enough to spend some time or money or thought on them.

An example: One spring I finished up three years with a group of middle school guys as their small group leader. I'd grown pretty close to these guys, and our group was all the good stuff you would hope a youth ministry small group could be. I wanted to give them something to speak into their lives, something they could keep beyond our final weeks.

So I made a craft! No, really, I did. I went to a landscaping place and bought a baseball-sized rock for each of them. Then I went to a craft store (yup) and bought a metallic paint pen. The whole thing cost me about six bucks. I thought long and hard about what particular character trait I saw emerging in each guy then wrote that trait on a rock.

They were two-word phrases, like:
• Ruthless Integrity
• Humble Leader
• Creative Ideator
• Uncompromising Focus
• Life-Giving Joy

When I handed out these gifts, I spent a few minutes describing how I saw each particular character trait emerging in the guy I gave it to. (By the way, when I later found out from a couple of their parents that their sons wanted to remember what I'd said to them but couldn't, I took the time to write those sentiments out and mail it to each of them.)

STOP READING!

———

Look, the reality is, this book isn't going to make you a great youth ministry small group leader. I mean, I hope you found some stuff helpful, and I hope you've been pushed to think in some new ways and have some ideas you're going to give a test run. But reading books only gets you so far.

Instead, there's a magic formula that will make you an absolutely stellar, off-the-charts-amazing, top-one-percent small group leader. Here's the magic formula:

- ➡ A grace-filled caring adult who's willing to be present to teenagers
- ➡ A small-ish group of teenagers
- ➡ The power of the Holy Spirit and presence of Christ

Result:
A freakin' awesome opportunity to impact the world.

That's the juice right there, baby. In other words, you have everything you need. Now stop reading and go call or text or otherwise engage a real-life teenager. Godspeed, and God's richest blessings on you and your ministry.